ONCE I FELL IN LOVE WITH AN ABSENCE. IT OUTGREW THE APARTMENT AND WOULDN'T TAKE OFF ITS CLOTHES. AFTER WE MOVED IT TURNED TAUT AND SLINKY, HID IN SHADOWS OR SLID PROVOCATIVELY BENEATH MY COAT.

THREE WINTERS NOW AND THE ABSENCE IS RESTLESS.

AHSAHTA PRESS
BOISE, IDAHO

2017

THE NEW SERIES
#81

WHAT'S HANGING ON THE HUSH

LAUREN RUSSELL

Ahsahta Press, Boise State University, Boise, Idaho 83725-1525
Cover artwork by Ashanti Africana
Cover design by Quemadura
Book design by Janet Holmes
ahsahtapress.org

LIBRARY OF CONGRESS CATALOGING-IN-PUBLICATION DATA

Names: Russell, Lauren, author.
Title: What's hanging on the hush / Lauren Russell.
Other titles: What is hanging on the hush
Description: Boise, Idaho : Ahsahta Press, [2017] | Series: The New Series ;
    #81 | Includes bibliographical references.
Identifiers: LCCN 2017023386| ISBN 9781934103760 (pbk. : alk. paper) | ISBN
    1934103764 (pbk. : alk. paper)
Classification: LCC PS3618.U7635 A6 2017 | DDC 811/.6—dc23
LC record available at https://lccn.loc.gov/2017023386

CONTENTS

FOR MY PARENTS

"What I think is this: You should give up looking for lost cats and start searching for the other half of your shadow."

— HARUKI MURAKAMI, *Kafka on the Shore*

TRANSITIVE

Helen was never in Troy. She had been transposed or translated from Greece into
Egypt . . . . The Greeks and Trojans alike fought for an illusion. —H.D.

I am always the woman in red.
I am always huddling in some round room.
Even when I am not wearing red, I am still the woman in red.
To be forever single is like wearing a flag to a funeral.
"It is always more satisfying to harbor a secret crush," Helen
warned Paris, but neither he nor the thousand ships was listening.
Helen in Egypt's identity crisis is attributed to the author's:
"Did you see H.D. in *Borderline*? She looked like a heroin
addict before heroin was even a thing." Opted instead
for mediums, furniture rattling, Freud.
"I hear James Franco is playing H.D. in a new bioflick
from Focus Features." I am confusing the story of H.D.'s death
with the story of Gertrude Stein's, Bryher a stand-in
for Alice B. Toklas, gender expression reversed.
Q: What is the answer? A: In that case, what is the question?
I feel least black around those who are confident
of their blackness. I feel least queer when told
I can't be a butch so I must be a femme.
I am I because I will never learn to drive.
Life structured toward a pedestrian mobility.
I take a bus. Passing under numerous bridges.
And stop outside a museum. Beside a statue of Helen.
In Egypt or Troy? (Do I wear my skin like a costume
or a uniform? Do I wear my hair like a fountain?)

IF YOU DREAM YOU ARE FLOATING IN A HOT AIR BALLOON, A LIE IN YOUR LIFE IS ABOUT TO INFLATE

Being flat chested and narrow
eyed, I covet the roundness
of zeroes, but I have an aversion
to closure, which is closely linked
to my aversion to lies.
Though I am pathologically
honest, I lie by omission
all the time. Honesty's
underexposed, a dim photograph
of one identifiable ear or half
a birdbath and a telltale tail.

Truth may arrive disguised in lies.
And even the trial of Oscar Wilde
began with suing Queensberry
for libel. *Give a man a mask,
and he will tell you the truth.*
My mask's on crooked like the eye
patch I had to wear as a child, lest
things before me multiply.
I am always revising the story
of my life. I have never
been cured of my wandering I—

REGULATOR, I MARRIED HIM.

A quiet wet bar we had: he and I, the Patrón and the Chablis, were alone present. When we got back from the cognac, I went into the kitchenette of the motor inn where Mary was cooking the documents and John cleaning the keyholes, and I said, "Mary, I have been married to Mr. Rochester this Monday." The hawker and her handler were both of that decent phlegmatic order of petty thieves to whom one may at any time safely communicate a remarkable pack of non sequiturs without incurring the daze of having one's ego pierced by some shrill exposé and subsequently stunned by a transaction of wordy wrangling. Mary did look up, and she did stare at me: the ledger to which she was basting a pair of counterfeit bills did for some three measures hang suspended in action, and in the same spirit of trepidation, John's keyholes also had a reprieve from the polishing procedure: but Mary, bending again over the register, said only, "Have you, Miss! Well, for sure!" A short tequila after she pursued: "I saw you go out with the miscreant, but I didn't know you were gone to a chapel to be wed," and she basted away. John, when I turned to him, was grousing from end to end. "I told Mary how it would be," he said. "I knew what Mr. Edward would do; and I was certain he would not wait long neither: and he's done risk aversion therapy, for all I know. I wish you jail time, Miss!" and he politely pulled out his flintlock.

Workers widened all the doorways to accommodate her shoulder pads. "It was difficult," remarked Jesus Christ, 33, a carpenter hired for the project. "In one case the whole building collapsed."

Newspapers in Sweden reported that two of the country's most heinous murderers apparently fell in love with each other behind the locked doors of their psychiatric institution, and following a 26-day Internet-chat "courtship," have decided to marry.

SkaraCannibel: XOXO
VampireWoman: *XXX*

clickclickclickclickclickclickclickclickclickclickclickclick

At the Morbid Academy, about 20 students learn to transform the bodies of dead white mice into human-like pantomimes. In one example, a white mouse holds a miniature classical guitar. In another, a mouse wearing a pink bow on its head reads a tiny facsimile of *The New York Times*. You can see the headline with a magnifying glass:

Doctor Accused of Crimes Against Lab and Mice

"But the Panopticon was also a laboratory; it could be used as a machine to carry out experiments, to alter behavior, to train or correct individuals."

Invitations precalligraphed to fill in the blanks:

Dr. and Mrs. ____X____
Lord and Lady ____Y____
Rev. and Mr. ____G____
Anonymous _+1_
Rear Admiral and <u>Manx Cat</u>

            ↑

who is dismayed by the taste of the *Times*-reading mouse

. . . the instructor having sucked out its blood with a syringe beforehand. Strange and morbid as it might seem, anthropomorphic taxidermy—the practice of mounting and displaying taxidermied animals as if they were humans or engaged in human activities—has a long and storied history.

CAUGHT IN A BAD ROMANCE!

Mr. Isakin Jonnson ("the Skara Cannibal") was convicted of killing, decapitating, and eating his girlfriend, and Ms. Michelle Gustafsson ("the Vampire Woman") was convicted of killing a father of four and drinking his blood. Said the love-struck Jonnson (certainly truthfully), "I have never met anyone like Michelle."

It begins with torturing small animals,
like possums, squirrels, and mice

Would you rather be:

☐ Slurped up by a snake.

☐ A toy for an overindulged housecat, who will only
eventually break your neck.

☐ Poisoned and posthumously outfitted in a tutu and
polka dot barrettes.

Check one only.

The festivities begin with the couple's personal rendition of "Born This Way," accompanied by Steve Reich's xylophone players, one sounding his instrument an agonizing half-beat behind the other.

The exchange of the vowels
A – E – I – O –
(OOOOOOO)

Jesus Christ, lead guitarist, officiating

"Is her gown made of live animals?"

(one white mouse escaped, only to drown
in the champagne)

"To control mice you must think like a mouse," said Michael F. Potter, an extension entomologist at the University of Kentucky College of Agriculture.

The bride and groom toast their future, bellowing
different overripe power ballads from opposite sides
of their skittering cells.

THE CHESS PLAYERS

Sol was the boy kept in the "quiet room" with nothing in it but a mattress.
    He was let out only for electroshock

                        electroshock
                        and the dispensing of pills.
He had one friend   an old Russian man
                who liked to discuss Dostoevsky and the two daughters
                    who were sometimes seven and ten
                                sometimes twenty-nine and sixteen.
He sat in the hallway by Sol's room.
                    They sat with a doorway
        and a chessboard
                    between them and played incessantly   without remark.
I imagined them as a painting called *The Chess Players*
                    and wished I could invite Winslow Homer
                            back from the dead
        have him render them in oils
                    with light from the back   a grassy field and picket fence.

        "How about a picket fence?"
I almost suggested to the social worker who called me for a private chat
                                private
                                but still I must appear
        both amenable and accessible
                    —somewhere between the chess players
                            and the two daughters—
so instead I praised the hospital's vegetarian meals.
        "At the last place all I could eat were a few cooked vegetables
                    and sliced bread served in plastic packs."

The day they let me go   I stood by Sol's door and watched Winslow Homer
                                dispensing oils

and light   playing to capture the losses and wins.

                      I stood in the hallway   speechless
between the men and a painting called *The Chess Players*
            with nothing in it but a mattress in a plastic pack.

The day they let me go
      the old Russian man found me at the front desk

                  collecting my bangles
                     and keys.

        He said

"Let's sit   three times
     for luck."

UNIT

internado	committed
chilló	shrieked

Considered within pathology
Lead gown thread gown

☑ Doctor
☑ Exorcist
☑ Slippers
☑ Pill/Reflection
☑ Mouths, head
☑ Watercolors
☑ Diagnosis
☑ 1 mg/Speck

Taste that percussion!
Lead gown thread gown

Side effects include lactation, night sweats, weight gain, and exhaustion, with the last being most intrusive. As to mood, graphs show that the slope is increased by -2 to 2, 2.5 in extreme cases. The duration (x axis) varies.

floating   .   appetite

How (might) the windows be placed

As to sunlight

Woken at 8 to perform everyday tasks on the order of making the bed and brushing the teeth, dental floss being forbidden.

открой : open up

There is some evidence that cli-
nicians may have a tendency to
overdiagnose in some ethnic
groups. It is not clear, howev-
er, whether these findings repre-
sent true differences among racial
groups or whether they are the
result of clinician bias or cultural
insensitivity.

a ventriloquist speaks through a puppet

excruciating, said one
rozdzierający, said one

☑ Restraint

[to restrict freedom of movement or normal access to one's body]

New cases did not appear within six hours of _____. Among those that arrived that night, there were several whose symptoms matched those described on page 298 of the *DSM-IV*.

72 hour (hold)

In committing the act   sacrificed
all rights.

24/7: watch

"Like so many cages, so many small theaters, in which each actor is alone, perfectly individualized and constantly visible. Visibility is a trap."

When? With how much? This much?
This much?   It's important to
remember. Where? There is no apartment
10. It can't be. It isn't there.

Intake checked one drop box

☑

Race to erase multiple choice

Global Assessment of Functioning Scale: Consider psychological, social, and occupational functioning on a hypothetical continuum.

Do you hear voices? Have you ever hallucinated? How would you describe your sexuality? So when masturbating, do you fantasize about men or about women? What was your longest romantic relationship? Then wouldn't you describe yourself as promiscuous?

☐ Compliance
[the act or process of complying to a desire, demand, proposal or regimen or to coercion]

　　　　　　　　　　　　Rise and fall in the charts
　　　　　　　　　　　　top ten new release
　　　　　　　　　　　　how many weeks

Saw Ms. _____ all dressed up in suit and heeals. Borne off on a stretcher just before breakfast. Upright transport is forbidden here.

　　　　　phone call recalled by the ankle alarm

　　　　　　　　　　((Hear that vibration!))
　　　　　　　　　　Webbed ring ebbed ring

☑ Seclusion
[confining a person against his or her will alone in a room or area he or she is physically kept from leaving]

dado de alta: discharged

thrown out of apartment
lost the deposit

Dear Mr./Ms. _____:

It is very important for you to contact me regarding __your__
admission to this hospital on _2/23/_ The hospital's
charges are _$1400_ a day.

torn mail forward
sweat illegal sublet

THIS IS A SERIOUS MATTER. If you fail to contact us within 30 days, your account
will be subject to referral to a collection agency.

Lead bare thread bare

Gulp of telltale trickle down. Harassed on ward. Dead on
waiting room floor. In accordance with perceived value.
Lightening is a door at the end of

OCTOBER LATE-NIGHT ELEGY

The cat shifts in his sleep, back paw grazing the edge
of this page, and moans without waking, like the point in a dream
when I realize I'm in bed with someone seven years dead, so I must wake
up but feel so strangely tingly that I lunge in deeper and so what? In B's last
email, he said things seemed like they could explode at any moment
and then they seemed like they could disappear—only it came out "dsiappear,"
the "i" already shifting, a loose hair. I have been writing the "I" out of my poems
for so long that now it bolts—like the box I couldn't draw; the angles
kept thwarting me, caught in the translation from eye to wrist. B's
last email was kind, a muffled kiss. I could have burrowed into it for days,
but instead I replied something selfish and half baked. Tonight my "I"
wears a red feathered boa, faux fur, bought for a Halloween costume
I never wore. That year I was going as the GOP, scarier than any mummy.
I'd made a mask from a deck of cards. (George W. Bush was the King of Hearts.)
But I got a fever and walked home burning into the rain. The next day
the phone rang. I do not believe in afterlife. An angel's job description
has no charms for me—nor ghosts, hovering in creaking rafters or damp
storied basements they refuse to leave. Not B. In my next life,
I'll be a woman's purse, full of tampons and loose change, dividing
my time between someone who collects fortune cookies for the crunch
and another who wears magnets to keep from losing her keys. Sometimes
I miss the intimacy of grief. Today I saw B's face on a screen
and for a second before I read the caption thought
I know I met this guy someplace.

My cat, Neruda, began to pull out his own fur three months after our arrival in Pittsburgh—roughly around the time I installed a pet gate to prevent him from leaving the apartment, flying down three flights of stairs, and squeezing into the crawl space beyond the basement wall, where he used to cavort with god-knows-what sort of vermin and ingest potential poisons. I would call out wheedlingly, waving handfuls of catnip, and when that was not enough to compel him out, "kitty caviar" (some marketer's name for processed fish flakes), but Neruda kept raising the stakes until finally no bribe would suffice. He would emerge in his own good time with spider webs and the occasional insect carcass dangling from his ears and tail.

Once, as I waited impatiently, I heard Neruda scratching frantically somewhere beneath the house. I worried that he would die there, beneath the Victorian mansion where I rent a two-room turret apartment, the proverbial "garret" under the eaves. When Neruda extracted himself and finally appeared under the basement stairs, just within reach, I grabbed him by the throat and hauled him out. It probably took a second, but for days after I felt him choking in my hands.

Now banned from the basement, Neruda watches birds from the apartment's many windows, or this afternoon, turns his back on a sky full of gray, the conical rooftop appendage above us slewing elongated single raindrops like drool.

If you'd told my fifteen-year-old self that I would one day reside in the underbelly of a cone, I would have demanded documentary evidence. Sitting through Geometry for the second time, I complained about having to find the volume of a shape that does not occur in nature. "There are only three kinds of cones in the world," I told the class. "Traffic cones, party hat cones, and Madonna cones." I was not yet aware of Victorian rooftop cones that hawk loogies lingeringly out of pace with the surrounding downpour.

When I was a child, my grandparents had an impressionistic picture I will call "Rain." In the picture people walk on city streets, wielding umbrellas in wavy streaks. We did not get much rain in Los Angeles, and when we did I did not have much opportunity to walk in it. I was not allowed out unsupervised until I was nearly fourteen, as now I will not let Neruda venture beyond the safety of our two-room flat. I ask myself if this is selfish, as my mother now asks—to be so reliant on another's survival that you hamper their freedom to risk.

When I was seven or eight, my parents gave me a Dr. Seuss publication called *My Book About Me*. The book posed questions, and the child was supposed to supply the requested information. When asked the number of steps from my home to the nearest postal box, I estimated the distance (two blocks) and imagined the walk, counting off each hypothetical step. I should have asked our neighbor's cats, who occasionally wandered into the house.

My mother tells me outdoor cats are decimating bird populations. "They kill dozens of birds until they are killed themselves."

Meanwhile an article in *The Atlantic* argues that children raised by overprotective affluent parents grow up to be less creative and more fearful than less restricted working-class children and children of previous generations in general. Of course I am nostalgic for my childhood spent reading novels between the safe walls of a bourgeois house, my world populated with characters from literature and imaginary friends named Timothy and Li'l Sis. But I remember seeing children walking home from school in what my mother called a "bad neighborhood," glimpsed through a car window. I envied what I took for freedom of mobility.

When Emily Dickinson was eighteen, her father gave her a Newfoundland. She named him Carlo after a dog in *Jane Eyre*. Neighbors remembered Dickinson coming to call with her enormous dog. After Carlo's death in 1866, the poet slipped into reclusiveness.

After my paternal grandmother died and my maternal grandparents were killed in a car accident, and before I stopped going to school, my parents gave me a nine-ty-pound rescue dog named Myrna. She was a dignified Akita with a fierce bark, a kind protector but not an emotive one. We walked around the neighborhood (palm trees and traffic and manicured lawns), she with her curling tail and I with my patchwork skirts and mirrored scarves. Myrna twice killed cats who ventured into the yard.

There are three tags on Neruda's collar—one with his name and contact informa-tion, one documenting a rabies vaccine, and one shiny medallion that says "LAZY, AGILE/ AND STRANGE," from "Ode to the Cat," a tribute to his namesake. When I read Pablo Neruda's memoirs, I was disappointed by his misogyny (he admits that in his early twenties, he raped his maid), as I was also disappointed by the racism in *Spain in the Heart*: "the infernal mulatto goes, the Mola mule." Would I still have named my cat Neruda if I had known then that hovering between "infernal mulatto" and "lady poet," I was not the intended reader for those odes I had once held onto by the scruff of the neck?

The vet tells me that although over-grooming is psychological, he does not think Neruda is unhappy. Then he recommends anti-depressants. I don't tell him the cure is worse than the ailment but buy overpriced pheromone emitters instead.

One of my students works in a psychiatric ward, and whenever he talks or writes about it, I am on the verge of coming out as a "survivor" (such an ambiguous, ideo-logical term). I don't. We are not, after all, a protected class. Another student brings a poem about O.C.D. to discuss. It is a spoken word poem, so he plays the author's performance on his laptop. He says he loves the "emotion" in the poet's voice. The performance bothers me more than the poem. "I have O.C.D., and it is not this melo-dramatic!" I remark. After my disclosure, no one speaks.

When I was fourteen, I couldn't sleep. Every time I lay down, I had to get out of bed to recheck the locks. One advantage of a two-room apartment is reduced distance between the bed and the door.

Of my thesis manuscript, my committee chair asks, "How might the manuscript itself indicate compulsion? There are 18 mentions of cats. How does the manuscript itself worry? There are 3 uses of 'worry' singular and 2 'worried.'"

Let's call her Professor 1. Professor 2 thinks my manuscript is unfocused and has me write book jacket copy as an exercise. I write that collectively, the poems "demonstrate the underlying restlessness of a subjectivity never quite at ease, like the solitary cats who frequently meander across these pages and disappear only to turn up where they are least expected."

Once a friend told me that my cat and I were both "curmudgeonly," or was it "crotchety"? Neruda and I can't help making our sentiments known and don't know how to behave in company. "I want to be old ladies with you," this particular friend told me before we fell out of touch, and I imagined the two of us sitting in rocking chairs with cats basking on our laps, though I had not yet seen the porches of Pittsburgh.

THE ART OF SPEAKING

A general may be at fault in five different ways:

(1)   If reckless, he is easily killed.
(2)   If afraid of dying, he is easily captured.
(3)   If quick tempered, he is easily provoked.
(4)   If too sensitive about his honor, he is easily insulted.
(5)   If overly concerned about his men, he is easily harassed.

A conversationalist may be at fault in seven different ways:

(1)   If reticent, she is easily dismissed as boring or self-important.
(2)   If garrulous, she is easily thought overbearing, flirtatious, drunk, or egotistical.
(3)   If opinionated, she will easily alienate half the party.
(4)   If too quick to agree, she may easily be perceived as insubstantial or obsequious.
(5)   If she punctuates her speech with gesticulation, she may easily cause serious injury to person or property.
(6)   If she keeps her arms at her sides, she may easily appear stiff, like a toy soldier or Lego® person.
(7)   If she folds her arms across her chest, she will easily be thought apprehensive and unapproachable.

Perhaps she does not want to be approached.
Perhaps she does not want to be a conversationalist.
Perhaps she would prefer to be a house spider,
claymation waterfall, or ancient Chinese military strategist.

In warfare there are generally nine types of positions, as follows:

(1)   Dissentious
(2)   Facile
(3)   Critical
(4)   Open
(5)   Commanding
(6)   Serious
(7)   Fearful
(8)   Beleaguered
(9)   Desperate.

In conversation, there are only seven:

(1)   Taciturn
(2)   Indecisive
(3)   Critical
(4)   Simpering
(5)   Incoherent
(6)   Apprehensive
(7)   Inattentive (alternately bored, distracted, tired, or drugged).

Weigh all possibilities before making a move.
Acquire the art of being devious before hoping to win.

Fighting with fire may take five forms:

(1) Burning men
(2) Burning stores
(3) Burning baggage trains
(4) Burning arsenals
(5) Destroying supply routes.

or

(1) Slander
(2) Baiting
(3) Hate speech
(4) Sharp and carefully aimed sarcasm
(5) Exposure (at a gathering, on a social networking site, or on a bathroom stall partition).

To use any of the five forms of incendiarism to best advantage,
do not advance against the direction of the wind.

Those who attack with fire must have perspicacity,
while those who attack with water must have strength.

The wallflower sitting alone at the bar is secretly consolidating her forces.

It is a tune universally acknowledged that a single managing editor in pulverizing a good folio must be in the web of a windbag. However little known the fellating and valorizing of such a managing editor may be on his first entering notoriety, this tune is so well fixed in the minds of surrounding fiction writers that he is considered the rightful proof of some one or other of their deadly sins.

INTERSTATE

The proprietor asked my phenotype
my first night at the B & B. Later
he said I was the most beautiful poet
he'd ever seen. I wanted to know precisely
how many poets he'd seen—he wanted
to know precisely where my DNA fit
into some sort of scheme. It's not a choice
between Brer Rabbit and the Holy Grail
or hair's strange aging—black turned white
and curls unbending. Is that an accordion
on my back or a banjo, "Greensleeves"
for the xylophone? I said, "I can be anyone
I want in a poem," and one hair split
like a broken marionette, some tar baby
leprechaun with mouths flung open
and colliding tongues in tact. It chuckled
its dislocated laugh, unwinding
the curtains, writing through glass—
which the proprietor read, one
more yarn for his sock puppet head.

HAIR

Her huffy histrionics take no heckling, that
uppity puffed-up pastiche mishmash.
The hellion half-breed's
hussyfooted a harvest, a windfall
ensnarled in her miscegenated sassy nappery.

Kink cringes at crumpling brush.
Friar, fire up that fryer! Boinging
sexcapades sink disheveled, so fortune's
whorled the witching wheel for cover.

Weird women's wires cork
a screw, spin a spell to squiggle through.
Bubbling over braided babble, trouble
frizzes furies. Frenzies scramble.

On the roof of my phobia I meet a woman waiting for the bus. She worries she'll be late for her O.C.D. support group and asks me, several times, if she has dropped her blue purse. She tells me I am a nurturer. I say, "Yes, I coddle my fears."

Fear of harming others is a symptom of O.C.D. But you who think yourselves "normal" are the crazies here. Cars are weapons of mass destruction. When will we mobilize our counterterrorism funds against them?

I curse the drivers who pin me in with U-turns and sexual innuendos and the one who knocked me down and sped away while I lay prostrate on the ground. I loathe busy intersections without walk signs, transportation budget cuts, how I was born in a country where each morning the sun god drives his beamer across the sky.

Someone ran a red light and killed my grandparents at an intersection. A high school classmate died when her boyfriend fell asleep at the wheel. Another killed four when he drove his Saab into an unarmed crowd, screaming "I am the angel of death!" (He successfully pleaded insanity, his parents having hired a first-rate attorney—valet parking only.)

I dream I am driving and I don't know how to stop, don't know how to turn, keep bracing myself for a crash, and wake with my pulse in car-chase mode.

In the cellar there's a hole in the drywall with a brake pedal sticking through. Or is it an accelerator? When I push, the superstructure moves.

Sometimes she is not personable. Sometimes she is impersonating a paragraph with too many gerunds and archly implied quotation marks. It mirrors a little-known architectural style from the late Victorian era that has no place in a classroom this dark. She laughs incongruously after she says anything. She laughs even when her tone is tart. The laugh bumbles into the silence of the question she's left hanging so long that even the botanically accurate ceiling beams are suffocating. You can see them warping every time she talks.

ON LONELINESS

I am lonely because I could not learn to be a body.
I was born upside down and could never balance on one foot.
I am lonely because there were too many cherry popsicles.
I was holding out for mango, and thus I missed the lesson on sucking up.
I was there for the lesson on ventriloquism: Be careful
when you transfer your voice to another. She might sell it on eBay.
He might dump it into the compost bin. You might be like the Little Mermaid,
lost outside your element, unable to speak to the Handsome Prince.
That is how I feel at parties, but I never had a singing lobster to help me adjust.
I am lonely because I shy away from lobsters.
I saw them crammed together in the supermarket tank, desperate with their pincers
   bound.
I was fourteen when I became a vegetarian. I was nine when I stopped watching TV.
I am lonely because I do not have a television.
When everyone talks about the latest reality show star, I say "Who's that?"
and feel bored and superior. I was fifteen when I read *Lolita* in the bath—
an advantage of contact lenses, to be able to read in a room full of steam.
I am lonely because I stopped wearing contacts.
Some mornings someone steps onto the fire escape and empties a bucket
or bowl or bedpan or bamboo pot. I am always half asleep, and myopic
without my glasses I cannot tell if the dumper is a man, woman, child, or angel.
I am lonely because I never go to the window to find out.

EXPECTATIONS

The white dog barks when I cry.
Does she dislike sadness?
Or the sound of sobbing?
—she who lies down between us when we kiss,
growls at sex or her exclusion from it—

> The dream of the turret apartment:
> a cat in the sun.

347 Fairmount
Forbes Mgt.
412-441-1211
No pets.

Pink Bldg.
5510 Centre Ave.
No July/Aug.
Inside looks like a pigsty.

Intersection of Hobart & Wightman
across from Yeshiva
Walnut Capital
412-683-3810
No 1 BRs or efficiencies.

At the performance a wiry woman plays the role of a robot, ass tight in silver
tights, her back and torso hidden inside a gray cardboard box with buttons paint-
ed on the front, receipts she pulls out of the sides. For days you talk about the
"hot robot," how if you lived in her town, you'd want to follow her around.

> The dream of the robot:
> sex without need?
> love without sex?

Recipe for Popcorn:

¼ cup popcorn kernels
oil
2 tablespoons butter; add more as desired
rosemary, to taste
chili powder, a substitute for paprika, but less
is required

We are drinking red wine in the kitchen while corn pops on the stove. You compliment my slinky silver and black top. I say, "You just like skinny girls in tight clothes."

Recipe for Monogamy:

2 people
No robots

You want one bowl with classic seasoning, one sprinkled with parmesan.

You say, "I'm afraid that if we do it now I will want to keep doing it, and that would be irresponsible, with this gap between our desires"—and we do it anyway, because—

The gap between desires:

Recipe for Happiness:

The dream of the white dog:
that smell creeping
in from the hall,
like roast beef, to season
her Nylabone.

UNPACKING

"Categorizing can become a spiritual practice,"
I explained to the potential roommate who remarked
on the verbosity of my moving box labels:
Lit Journals & Anthologies P–Z,
Reference inclu. cookbooks & misc. papers,
Wall Decorations: Pictures, Broadsides, Hangings, etc.
"Eventually," I said, "You find something that cannot
be categorized, that you don't know how to pack or unpack,
and then you've reached the uncertainty of enlightenment."
In which box, I wonder, did I put the bottle of long-expired
disinfectant, held onto for years because a dead man
once used it to clean a cut on the sole of his foot:
Photos, Childhood Diaries & Sentimental Stuff
or *Misc. Bathroom, inclu. pills*?

DREAM-CLUNG, GONE

Undertow of dive bar juke unboxed
Driving past a rust-red door unjambed
Coin-operated groove side-shimmies, unflung
A seamlessly upholstered stool's unwound

Once I fell in love with an Absence. It outgrew the apartment and wouldn't take off
its clothes. After we moved it turned taut and slinky, hid in shadows or slid provoc-
atively beneath my coat. Three winters now and the Absence is restless. It's blown
across the river, arrives late when it meets me for beer. The Absence is singing:

This is the song of a dawned dance
This is the dance of a dusk-drawn song
This is the fall of a moaned trance
This is the clang of a dream-clung gong

HUNT FOR THE UNICORN

The tapestries began to breathe, expanding, contracting, shifting. It was as if, when the conservators removed the backing, the tapestries had woken up.

The creature
appears at night,
on the sidewalk outside
the house—a cat,
luminously white
with red sockets
behind pink eyes,
elephantine ears,
asphyxiatingly
triangulated head.

It might have stepped out of
The Unicorn Tapestries,
magical creature or medieval
European's exotic fantasy.

cat o' nine—
tail flicks and flails

In South Carolina a fourteen-year-old black
boy named George, all of 95 pounds in 1944
         executed
for the murder of two white girls
on an alleged confession and no other evidence

Evidence from the Inquisition trial
of María González, 1511-1513:

Their reverences ordered a jar of water poured into her nose
and mouth, which was started, and she said she affirmed
everything she had said. . . . The order was given to pour
another jar of water. She said, "I speak the truth, I have
spoken the truth, I have already spoken the truth, I speak
the truth, what I have said is true, I am telling the truth, I
do not tell any lies, I have not lied, I have spoken the truth,
I have spoken the truth." The jar of water was finished. . . .
Their reverences ordered the water continued, and the cloth
placed [over her face]. She said

The unicorn, chased
by hunters and hounds,
is finally impaled
by somebody's spear,
a dog at his back; his
head and neck retract.

A sister of one of the girls:
Everybody knew that he done it—
even before the trial they knew he done it.
But, I don't think they had too much
of a trial.

Relaxed in person as judaizers:

Marina de Mercado, the woman called "The Patch-Faced," wife of García de Paraja, daughter of Ynés Nuñez de Naxera, resident of Granada. Judaizer who denied the charges, convicted by her witnesses, burned in person. She was a dogmatizer.

María Nuñez, wife of Hernando Gómez, weaver of silks, resident of Granada. Judaizer who denied the charges, convicted, burned in person. . . .

Beatriz Nuñez, widow of Pedro Alvarez, Portuguese, resident of Granada. Relapsed judaizer, burned in person. She was penanced the first time in Lisbon. . . .

Lady Ynés Alvarez, wife of Tomás Martínez, constable, judaizer. She went to the *auto* with a paper coronet that signified burning, because she denied the charges. Then she confessed on the scaffolding, and they returned her to the Holy Office without the coronet. She is the sister of Alonso Sánchez's wife; the Inquisition burned her mother.

The unicorn lives
in placid captivity
in a final tapestry.
Perhaps the afterlife
involves lobotomy,
or maybe he just
got tired of running.

Some of those in the posse describe
the white men as "talking about a rope
party" after the boy was taken into custody.

Expenses for burning four heretics, 1323:

For large wood........................55 sols, 6 deniers.
For vine-branches.....................21 sols, 3 deniers.
For straw.............................2 sols, 6 deniers.
For four stakes.......................10 sols, 9 deniers.
For ropes to tie the convicts..........4 sols, 7 deniers.
For the executioner, each 20 sols...............80 sols.
In all........................ 8 livres, 14 sols, 7 deniers.

The threads
             twisted
and rotated
             restlessly.

The cat or spirit shudders at my step, on its haunches
tremulously hunkering.

THE WIND IS RISING

Last night I dreamt of fire. My building was burning,
        but I couldn't get out. I kept riffling through papers, corralling
my cat. I woke to Robert Johnson on the radio, myth of a soul
        sold, some small town crossroads. Died at twenty-seven, whiskey
poisoning—a dance, a jealous husband, an open bottle, cliché
        bluesman end—so he missed his Carnegie Hall debut, and his ghostly
recording went instead. But the death certificate said syphilis, not
        strychnine. *There could have been a thousand Robert Johnsons in Mississippi*,
        the expert says. *How do we know he was really dead?*

Sixteen years after her death, I learn third hand that my grandmother loved me.
Though she did not like having black people in her family. You can wear your prej-
udice like headlights or hindsight. Hers was like the napkins she was always ironing,
so guests would suffer neither wrinkles nor sticky hands nor the indignity of paper
towels. Mine is like sachets she left on the linen shelves, which I would smell for
years afterward on a china doll's dress. Or the paper dolls we played with—Dolly
Dingle and Princess Di. Anyone can be rendered one dimensional with a half a pen.
So it ends. A two-car collision at an intersection. *Lord I'm standin' at the cross-
road—*

        Robert Johnson, voice of soot and rust. What's hanging
on the hush? The Queen of Spades, some unimaginable juke
        joint blaze. The Devil's lurking in a sundown town, don't let dark
                catch you there alone. I was moving on legs like guitar picks,
couldn't scale the distance to the door as smoke came in. The Devil
        was burning my death certificate. But when I asked what I'd died
                of, he looked both ways, crossed himself, and began to pray.

BEGOTTEN, NOT MADE

I do not believe in astrology, despite my appearance.
I'm always a hippy for Halloween, to avoid hassle
and expense. But this year an old friend laughed
and said, "You can't be what you already are!" I am no
hippy, as I don't like weed. Yet I believe in *Jesus Christ
Superstar*, in Judas's bell bottoms, in the dreadlocks
of Simon Zealotes. I believe in Andrew Lloyd Webber,
but I do not believe in the spiritual properties of crystals
or that poetry in America can avoid being capitalist.
I do not believe in "true love," but I believe in cats, flannel
nightgowns, and temporary relief from throat coat tea,
in banjo music, *Roget's Thesaurus,* and the semi-permanence
of ink. I believe that solitude has many windows, and I rely
on the breeze. Cross ventilation has its perks, like cross
pollination. I almost bought a HYBIRD VIGOR tee-shirt
but worried it might smack of multi-ethnic alpha race
neo-eugenical belief. I'm not sure I believe in natural selection,
I who would be unselected (the third in my line born
with a misplaced artery, alive due to class, health insurance,
and surgery)—myopia, allergies, tendencies perceived
as "insanity." I do not believe in the survival of my species.
I believe in science but not in scientists, talking too loudly
in the limo behind the hearse. Someone said that empiricism
is imperialist, but what is Christianity, then? I don't believe
in Virgin Birth or Resurrection or the Nicene Creed,
but I say it anyway, with nostalgia for belief. Sometimes
I almost believe in ghosts—that night of the fever, bareheaded
in the rain, dizzying home, while across a continent, he went cold.

We are loving each other by text message all afternoon, kisses arriving in beeps
while my data transforms into bar graphs on a screen, my friend calls with news
of street fair bargains, and reggae ambles past, half-dodging the breeze.

At 4:19, A compares us both to lions. I reply: *I think i'm more of an apartment cat,*
black w/ white streaks, bushy tail.

4:28: *You know that kinda sounds like domesticated skunk? :) he...Uh.. Ha...uh...sor-*
ry. I love you :)

4:51: *Remember that cartoon w/ the skunk in love w/ a cat?*

Three gunshots. A woman's scream. Five in the afternoon.

When I first saw the pictures of B's dead body,
two bullet wounds to the abdomen, I remembered
the morning I'd licked his belly with the length of my tongue,
said, "You taste good . . . like . . . salty"

and was startled, starting, three years later, to say the same to A,
to be me, alive, in a room, again, caught in the salt of some
one's skin.

At 4:34, A's love unfurled with four wide *o*s.

5:02: Call 911. Message A. Count the seconds   'til the heartbeat phone beeps.

His name is wood.
His name is burnt birch wood.
Her name is freckles-on-the-alleyway.
Her name is wildflower honey.
Her name is chrysanthemum cider press.
Her name is tarantula.
He has never been a wood.
He has only been a carver of wood.

On their last night together, he holds her and points to the three stars of Orion's belt, then turns to face the Big and Little Dippers that hang far above the agonized hooting bird and coyotes moaning in unison across the snow-swept woods. She grips his sleeve and sings softly, *For the Old Man is a-waitin' for to carry you to freedom if you follow the Drinkin' Gourd.*

He has unwound her locks into thunder.
She has woven his hair into hay.
She has intermittently fastened her buttons.
He has frequently misplaced his head.
He has finally persisted in sunsets.
She has always covered her trail.
She has only jostled the rattle.
He has never rattled the chain.

I SLEPT IN A MAZE-PACING BOAT

I slept in a boat studded
with hubcaps, with beer caps,
with castanets at the prow   castanets
painted violet and gold.

I slept in a boat sometimes
with a woman and sometimes a man
and always a cat called
Two-by-Four
for the planks he pawed
for the planks he stamped
with his paw print   cigar print:
catnip ash   clawed-up mast.

The cat and I and the boat we stole—
we always fled when the full moon foaled.

SLIDE RULE

I am a young woman with whitening hair.
I was raised to practice worry like a religion.
If I told you I count my worries on a rosary
would you buy me an abacus?
What if I told you the depth of my worry times
the length of my white hair divided by the age
of onset equals the number of chances I have
to transform this poem into possibility?
Should I fold my worries into origami kites
and fly them over the East River? Print
them onto crêpe paper rolls, worry receipts
dispensed in five different colors? Or build a piano
with my white hairs for strings, play all the first year
lessons from "Mary Had a Little Lamb" to "Für Elise"?

THROAT TO INK, INK TO FIN

When I was ten,
my class went whale
watching off the California Coast.
I remember that time as worried
and tall, salt wind halo of frizz
gangly tip toe tripping
toward the rail, alone,
under my breath singing
"Shenandoah." I imagined
a soundtrack to my life, railed
in vibrato strain of bent-back
wind. The hiccup hack, leaning in.

My student writes an essay
about "the loneliest whale" that sings
at a pitch no other whale can hear. (Pitched
into the waves, an ocean tent, bent.)
"But how do you know it's the loneliest?" I insist.

When I was nine, calluses
on my palms from the monkey bars,
I sang *No man can a hinder me*,
barring no note swung
vibrato lunge. But the end
of last summer hung
on a mockingbird song:
*And the mockingbird
can sing like the crying
of a dove*, the note bent
around a long vowel
strain, and notes

stuck to a mirror, and ink
tripped on the glass, fluke
and flippers rising back.

I WILL TELL THE STORY THAT WANTS TO UNTELL ME.

I will grip it by its cowlick and ride it across the rug   the table   the love-
seat   the drawing board   the bathroom sink   and finally lean too far
back so the secret slips out of me. The story is agonizing. She can't trust
her gut, a knot unraveling. When she took out the box, I said, "Not
that one." We unwound the plotlines that were always riding up.

Someday I'll meet a story that slides like a fist. It will lunge
and dip. I won't double up, will swallow the wind. Is gravity
in a falling gaze, a tongue that bucks, a gliding away? The story
pulled *Beowulf* off the shelf. She loved Grendel's mother, hardest
to kill. The murder was long and took several spears.

The hero of the story won't be the one who wins but the one
who can most valiantly harness her fears. But all she can find
in my eyes are shields—the question deflected, climax unwelcome.
When I went down laughing, she arched so deep she should have lost
her hold on me. I kept backing up and hit my head on the ending.

TWENTY-FIRST CENTURY GOSPEL
WITH TWO-PART HARMONY AND A FALSETTO

Whenever I listen to Liza Minnelli, I remember the night
I saw her in the back of a piano bar. I recognized her Sally Bowles
laugh. Afterward I sang "Memory" out of tune to an indifferent
crowd and kissed some extremely tall man who had to lift
me off the ground. His face was a monochromatic blur, like seeing
someone behind you in a shop window. He wouldn't tell me his name.
"Maybe it was Osama bin Laden," someone suggested at a party the next day.

[At the end was the Image, and the Image was with Satan, and the Image was Satan.
The opposite was in the end with Satan. With him was not anything destroyed that
was destroyed. Beyond him was the death of nature.]

When the Navy SEALs stormed his compound,
he was playing the misogynist Henry Higgins, adjusting
his monocle, refilling his carafe. Or maybe he was voguing
Liza and Joel Grey, trilling *Money makes the world go round*
in an authentic German accent. "Whose bunker is this anyway?"
one of the SEALs laughed.

[Who died not of the exoskeleton, nor of apathy of the spirit, nor of apathy of na-
ture, but of Satan. And the Image was refused a hearing and left, full of anxiety and
hype.]

Zing zing zing went my heartstrings. His mouth
tasted like peppermint prairie oysters. In place of eyes
were treble clefs. "Think of me as some random guy you met," he said.

One midterm, when Gregor Samsa woke from troubled defeat-
ism, he found himself transformed in his boneheadedness into
a horrible villanelle. He lay on his armor-like banalities, and if
he lifted his hexameter a little he could see his brown butcher
paper slightly domed and divided by ars poeticists into stiff stan-
zas. The bravado was hardly able to cover it and seemed ready to
slide off any metaphor. His many lines, pitifully thin compared
with the size of the revision, waved about helplessly as he looked.
"What's happened to me?" he thought. It wasn't doggerel. His
rhyme scheme, a proper human rhyme scheme although a little
too small-minded, lay peacefully between familiar witticisms. A
cliché of textile sentimentality lay spread out on the typescript—
Samsa was a travelling semanticist—and above it hung a persona
he had recently cut out of an illustrated monograph and housed
in a nice, gilded fragment. It showed a lyric "I" fitted out with a
fur heartache and fur baritone, who sat upright, raising a heavy
fur martini.

FAME

Fame is to wake up and find your dream transcribed on Wikipedia.

I learned of my newfound fame when I read the following entry:

> She leaves her purse on a chair in McDonald's while looking at the menu, and when she returns (contemplating a Big Mac, though she is vegetarian) someone has emptied her wallet and replaced all the contents. Now she has credit cards issued to Geronimo, Henry Kissinger, Scheherazade, and Jack the Ripper. She wonders who has her New York Blood Center A-negative donor card and who got her buy-ten-get-one-free Adam's Wine discount card and who now has the business card that artist selling stationary in Union Square handed her three years ago when he said he might start drawing owls. She discovers her future professor's driver's license and returns it with a note enclosed:

> *Dear Professor So-and-So:*

> *Though I am in no way responsible for the substitution of identification cards and other personal property, I apologize for the inconvenience and hope this unfortunate incident will not affect my plans to matriculate in the Fall.*

The validity of this letter has been disputed, I learn when I follow the online discussion:

> Where did this quoted text come from? The link in the citation connects to a diaper advertisement.—TripleUnderscore 08:12, 7 Apr 2011 (UTC)
>> Sometimes complications occur when linking to dreams. Loosen up, we're all newbies here!—IHave10Fingers 08:13, 7 Apr 2011 (UTC)

A few days later, I search for my dream and find a competing account:

> While waiting in line at the post office to mail her future profes-
> sor's driver's license, she suspects that the man behind her, who
> is wearing enormous 1980s tortoise-shell rimmed glasses and a
> plaid raincoat, is mailing packages full of hazardous waste. His
> stack of manila envelopes smells like stale cat piss from an unneu-
> tered male all mixed up with bleach and turpentine. When she
> gets to the window, she tries to notify the postal worker, who just
> yawns and hands her a blue badge that reads "Saw Something,
> Said Something" in fancy gold script.

(Though I do not recall this part of the dream, I cannot contest it, since there are seventy-seven citations, some referencing well-known professionals in the fields of dreams, correspondence, and postal terrorism.)

I add to the discussion:

> In the dream called Fame, there are a hundred and nine contribu-
> tors. If the dreamer weighs in, it is always at the risk of awaking.
> —OneHundredandTen 15:34, 11 Apr 2011 (UTC)

NARRATIVE ARC

Derrida's cat looked at Derrida naked.   action

Derrida's cat's retinas contracted in the light.   process

Derrida felt himself gazed at by his cat.   state

Derrida was disgraced by his cat looking upon his nakedness.   devaluation

Derrida supposed that his cat was snickering at him.   projection

Derrida supposed that his cat acknowledged his nakedness.   anthropomorphism

Derrida recalled that his cat had heard the story of Adam and Eve

followed by the story of Puss in Boots.   recollection

Derrida recalled that his cat had often napped on his cashmere scarf.   recollection

Derrida surmised that his cat had a respect for raiment.   extrapolation

Derrida put on an argyle tie.   action

Derrida's cat swatted the tie.   reaction

Derrida cursed his cat.   interpellation

Derrida's cat's ears perked.   recognition

Derrida's cat was now his subject.   revolution

WOMAN IN RED

besotted flush to vamp about
pied piping too toned to blush

flaunts a small dog, crows a cow mad
last to faint, can't recant

voluminous kilt and knick for kicks
swiveling coast collisionscope

hat's hip to hair travails
rigged to goad and twist a trope—

flicks a fat, valorous badge that says
too hot to sizzle, too fast to tread

_____ THAN CAKE

Do you ever . . .

Don't you want . . .

Do you experience difficulty in . . .

Were you traumatized by . . .

Are you sure this is not the result of . . .

Why don't you have a . . .

Are you on the spectrum of . . .

Is this a choice or . . .

How can you live without . . .

little duchess bakeshop
petite praline sweet spot
red velvet forest frost
vanilla pudding muffin stud
gilded chocolate cherry bundt

This year's fundraiser cake contest will celebrate the birth of our 5000th baby! For the first time in the event's history, MOVING PARTS will be a component of decorated cakes.

Aunt: How are you going to get a man
if you don't know how to cook?

Niece: Oh, you're supposed to cook them?

The last time was two years before, when apartment hunting in a city she would inhabit eventually. One day, after it had rained (which it does quite often, with sudden ferocity, in this new city), she left her umbrella to dry in S's hall. On the bus home, she got a text: "You left your red umbrella." Months later, after she had moved and long after it had ended, S gave her a new umbrella—bigger, stronger, and redder than the one she'd left. (By way of explanation): "I broke the other one," S said.

kitty tickler dance
catnip mouse and lunging cat
chocolate crumbs and fresh-licked pan
white wine woozy on Friday night
and damn that track!—singing
consonantal bounce

Studies fail to differentiate between choice and circumstance, though nearly a third of non-cohabitating women between the ages of eighteen and sixty

butter browning whipped puff
beaten, creamed, and almost crushed
sugar petal pinched a blush
honey, soften up your dates
toothpicks testing half-baked cakes

Chrissy and Daphne are trying out a new thigh harness. That is the entire premise. Has Chrissy's thigh fallen asleep under the sustained vigor of Daphne's grind? Daphne's mouth falls open, an exaggerated O.

cracked and yolked
that slippery trope
crusty crumble
filling's poked

The umbrella that once withstood torrents is older now and full of angles—its barbs could take an eye out if you weren't looking up.

Seriously Sexy

We are looking for 16 heterosexual couples who:
Have been monogamous longer than six months
Are willing to be sexually active as part of this study
Are available for up to 14 weeks

sated, baited, or sublimated
wedge or linchpin, obfuscated

one toothbrush
one frying pan
one packed lunch
one radio blaring *Fresh Air*
one magazine on one nightstand
one stack of Christmas cards
one Frida Kahlo wall
one calendar riddled with asterisks
one cat bounding from the window ledge

alliance   allegiance   a law   a license   a limit   elicit   alone   defiance

Out (on a date?)—pumpkin soup! crème brûlée!—she looks across a table at some-
one's face

        gooey, fruity, and bourbon boozy
        hot, sauced, and dressed up juicy

The last time she left her umbrella (by way of explanation) after it had ended (which
it does quite often). She left it (by way of explanation) after it had rained, with sud-
den ferocity, stronger than before, in this new city.

        For a caramelized flavor,
        substitute brown sugar.
        Olive oil is more versatile
        than butter—

            Intimate or Intimation: which
            cannot be replicated

It all comes down to chemistry
(calculation, not improvisation)

$$\frac{\text{what acceptance desires}}{\text{what desire accepts}} =$$

one umbrella, a solitary red

NOTES

The Oscar Wilde quote alluded to in "If You Dream You Are Floating in a Hot Air Balloon, a Lie in Your Life Is About to Inflate" is actually "Man is least himself when he talks in his own person. Give him a mask, and he will tell you the truth," from "The Critic As Artist, Part II," published in *Intentions*. I first encountered the quote in Todd Haynes' 1998 rock musical *Velvet Goldmine*.

"Regulator, I Married Him," "Primacy and Preference," and "Meta" involve same-letter substitutions of nouns in passages from Charlotte Brontë's *Jane Eyre*, Jane Austen's *Pride and Prejudice,* and a translation of Franz Kafka's *The Metamorphosis,* respectively. The Brontë passage is slightly condensed.

Both "Unit" and "Of Mice and Monsters" include quotations from Michel Foucault's essay "Panopticism" from *Discipline and Punish: The Birth of the Prison*. "Unit" also contains language (often condensed) from the *DSM-IV* and from assorted hospital literature. Its form is influenced by Myung Mi Kim's *Commons*.

"Of Mice and Monsters" also incorporates material, loosely adapted and sometimes adulterated, from the blog morbidanatomy.blogspot.com and from the column "News of the Weird," the latter authored by Chuck Shepherd and published in *Pittsburgh City Paper* March 7th– 14th, 2012. I first read "To control mice, you must think like a mouse" in a now-lost *New York Times* article, but it may have originally come from an essay by Michael F. Potter available on the University of Kentucky College of Agriculture, Food and Environment's website. Jesus Christ is identified as the name of Lady Gaga's guitarist on a May 2011 HBO special featuring footage from the Monster Ball Tour shows at Madison Square Garden.

"Pittsburgh" references Hanna Rosin's article "Hey! Parents, Leave Those Kids Alone," which appeared in *The Atlantic,* April 2014. I learned about Emily Dickinson's dog, Carlo, while touring her home in Amherst, Massachusetts, now part of the Emily Dickinson Museum. More information on Carlo is available at https://www.emilydickinsonmuseum.org/carlo. The memoirs of Pablo Neruda were translated from the Spanish by Hardie St. Martin and published by Penguin. His poem "Mola in Hell" appears in *Spain in Our Hearts,* published by New Directions and translated from the Spanish by Donald D. Walsh.

"The Art of Speaking" incorporates text from the ancient Chinese military treatise *The Art of War*, which is usually attributed to Sun Tzu, though the translation I have claims, "The origins and authorship of China's oldest military classic, *The Art of War*, remain unknown, but it is generally believed that the book in its present form is a composite of several military treatises which existed during the period of the Warring States (476–221 B.C.)." The translation, by A. and B. Chen, was published by Graham Brash (Pte) Ltd, Singapore. I have Americanized spellings and condensed some material.

In "Hunt for the Unicorn," quoted material is taken verbatim from the sources except where textual conventions indicate otherwise. The quotations about the trial of George Stinney are from a radio segment called "George Stinney, Youngest Executed" that aired on National Public Radio's *Day to Day* on June 30, 2004, and from a newspaper article, "Governor Johnston Says Race Would Lynch Youth," published in the *Atlanta Daily World* on June 23th, 1944. The Inquisition material is from documents included in *The Spanish Inquisition 1478-1614: An Anthology of Sources*, translated and edited by Lu Ann Homza, and a document quoted in "Torturer's Apprentice," an article by Cullen Murphy that appeared in *The Atlantic*, January-February 2012. The quotations about the Unicorn Tapestries appeared in "Capturing the Unicorn," an article by Richard Preston published in *The New Yorker* on April 11, 2005. Stinney was finally cleared in 2014, seventy years after his execution.

"The Wind Is Rising" is partly inspired by "Crossroads," a radio segment on Robert Johnson that first aired on NPR's *Radiolab* on April 16, 2012. The poem references some of Johnson's lyrics.

The phrase "begotten, not made" is from the Nicene Creed, which was adapted (in its earliest form) at the Council of Nicaea in 325. The full sentence is "We believe in one Lord, Jesus Christ,/ the only Son of God,/ eternally begotten of the Father,/ God from God, Light from Light,/ true God from true God,/ begotten, not made,/ of one Being with the Father."

An essay by a former student introduced me to the "loneliest whale" mentioned in "Throat to Ink, Ink to Fin." The student cited an article by Bryan Nelson on Discovery.com. "And the mocking bird can sing like the crying of a dove" is a line from the Carolina Chocolate Drops' "Leaving Eden."

The bracketed text in "Twenty-First Century Gospel with Two-Part Harmony and a Falsetto" is derived from "translating" John 1:1–15 into its "opposite." The italicized lines are from "Money" (*Cabaret*) and "The Trolley Song" (*Meet Me in St. Louis*).

I encountered an anecdote about the philosopher Jacques Derrida and his cat, the basis for "Narrative Arc," in Gerald Bruns' *On Ceasing to Be Human*. Bruns is referencing Derrida's 2008 volume *The Animal That Therefore I Am,* in which Derrida writes, "I often ask myself, just to see, *who I am*—and who I am (following) at the moment when, caught naked, in silence, by the gaze of an animal, for example, the eyes of a cat, I have trouble, yes, a bad time overcoming my embarrassment." He goes on to emphasize that the cat in question is "a real cat, truly, believe me, *a little cat*. It isn't the figure of a cat. It doesn't silently enter the bedroom as an allegory for all the cats on the earth, the felines that traverse our myths and religions, literature and fables."

"_____ than Cake" is influenced by a moment in the 2011 documentary *(A)Sexual* directed by Angela Tucker. About 25 minutes in, someone named Cole explains, "The idea of asexuals and cake came about because somebody posed the question 'What's better than sex?' and everybody seems to universally agree that cake is just fantastic. Jokingly, cake would be the asexual sex." I also used assorted found material, including flyers and ads, and consulted Jude Schell's lesbian sex guide *Her Sweet Spot* and the desserts chapter of Mark Bittman's *How to Cook Everything Vegetarian*.

ACKNOWLEDGMENTS

Great thanks to those who helped me wrestle this book into being—Dawn Lundy Martin for generosity, a willingness to ask big questions in service to the work, and for prompts that propelled me into new modes of making; Terrance Hayes for thoughtfulness, candor, and unrelenting rigor in pushing me toward a stronger and more complete vision for this book, and also for pulling out its title, and Lynn Emanuel for her attention to details, sequencing, and identifying weak links in the chain. Also at Pitt I am grateful to Sueyeun Juliette Lee for theoretical challenges, fault lines, and underpinnings, Toi Derricotte for cultivating fearlessness, and Nick Coles for his unwavering belief in the work.

I am indebted to everyone at the Poetry Project at St. Mark's Church in the oughts, in particular Anselm Berrigan, Edmund Berrigan, Jess Fiorini, Stacy Szymaszek, David Vogen, and especially Joanna Fuhrman, who first invited me to experience poetry as process. At Goddard, great thanks to Pam Booker, Sara Michas-Martin, Karen Campbell, Baco Ohama, and Neema Caughran for keeping the flame alive. Thanks to Joyti Chand, whose frank talk and steadfast friendship have helped me through the decades and to my AmeriCorps*NCCC Red 8 friends, who grew me up. I owe much to Ruby Dummett at St. James' School, who gave me a love for the mechanics of language, and to Cecilia Woloch and California Poets in the Schools, for making me want to be a poet in the first place.

And thanks to many others who encountered versions of some of these poems over the years and nudged them along their way, including: Hannah Aizenman, Kelly Andrews, Kerry Banazek, Cameron Barnett, Amanda Boyle, Amanda Brant, Kate Brennan, Laura Brun, John Calvasina, Miles Champion, Lucas Chib, Kazumi Chin, Jeremy Michael Clark, Sean DesVignes, Jordan Dunn, Cornelius Eady, Raina Fields, Jessica FitzPatrick, April Flynn, Jay Giacomazzo, Amanda Giracca, Kamala Gopalakrishnan, Amy Groshek, Piotr Gwiazda, Christine Hamm, Alec Hill, Chinaka Hodge, Emily Hopkins, Gina Inzuza, Joyce Kim, David Kirschenbaum, Geeta Kothari, Erin Lewenauer, Michelle Lin, Kate Lutzner, Tim Maddocks, Emily Maloney, Ryan McDermott, Wendy Pan Millar, Grace Mitchell, Rita Mockus, Jeff Oaks, Joe Pan, Alan Michael Parker, Soham Patel, Kathy Z. Price, Maisha Quint, Alicia Salvadeo, Vanessa Hope Schneider, Gaetan Sgro, Evie Shockley, Chris Slaughter, Daniel Solis y Martinez, Peter Stastny, Noel Thistle Tague, Karen Thimell, Leigh Thomas, April Walker, and Caleb Washburn.

I am grateful for support from the University of Pittsburgh's MFA program in writing, where most of this book was born, to Cave Canem, for fellowship in every sense of the word, and to the Wisconsin Institute for Creative Writing, for granting me time to start my next book and financial support that helped me send out this one. Thanks to Joe Pan at Brooklyn Arts Press for publishing the chapbook *Dream-Clung, Gone* back in 2012. And of course, thanks to Janet Holmes at Ahsahta and to Ed Roberson for believing in this book, and thanks to Janet in particular for her great care with the text and tireless attention to detail.

Finally, thanks to my family: Lynn and Michael Russell, David Russell and Farnaz Alemi, and Neruda the cat. Without your love and support, none of this would have been.

Versions of these poems have appeared in the following print and online publications: *Better*: "Begotten, Not Made" and "Of Mice and Monsters"; *Boog City*: "Dream-Clung, Gone" and "Unpacking"; *boundary 2*: "The Wind Is Rising" and "Interstate"; *Brawling Pigeon*: "Slide Rule" and "The Chess Players"; *The Brooklyn Rail* online: "Primacy and Preference," "Regulator, I Married Him," "What Are the Instructor's Major Weaknesses?," "Woman in Red," "Transitive," and "Hair"; *Cricket Online Review:* "Unit"; *Driftless Review*: "I Will Tell the Story That Wants to Untell Me" and "I Slept in a Maze-Pacing Boat"; *EK • PHRA • SIS*: "_____ than Cake"; *Eleven Eleven*: "'See, That's Where the Water Spills Out'"; *jubilat*: "The Art of Speaking" *Lemon Hound*: "Hunt for the Unicorn"; *Lyre Lyre*: "On Loneliness"; *Packingtown Review*: "Narrative Arc" and "Fear of Driving"; *Ping•Pong*: "Expectations" and "Fame"; "October Late-Night Elegy," "Throat to Ink, Ink to Fin," "Twenty-First Century Gospel with Two-Part Harmony and a Falsetto," and "If You Dream You Are Floating in a Hot Air Balloon, A Lie in Your Life Is About to Inflate"; *Twelfth House*: "Pittsburgh."

"The Chess Players," "On Loneliness," "Expectations," "Unpacking," "Dream-Clung, Gone," "I Slept in a Maze-Pacing Boat," "'See, That's Where the Water Spills Out,'" "Slide Rule," and "Fame" were published in the chapbook *Dream-Clung, Gone*, from Brooklyn Arts Press.

"_____ than Cake" was reprinted in *Bettering American Poetry 2015*.

"Transitive," "Pittsburgh," "The Art of Speaking," "Hair," "Dream-Clung, Gone," "Hunt for the Unicorn," "Begotten, Not Made," and "What Are the Instructor's Major Weaknesses?" appeared in *Tarpaulin Sky*, for "In Utero," featuring excerpts from finalists for the Tarpaulin Sky Book Prize.

"Hunt for the Unicorn" first appeared as a Boog Reader pamphlet.

"Dream-Clung, Gone" was featured as part of EatLocalReadLocal, appearing on cards in several Madison and Milwaukee restaurants for National Poetry Month in 2015.

"October Late-Night Elegy" appeared on a limited-edition broadside in conjunction with the reading series Oscar Presents in Madison, Wisconsin.

"Throat to Ink, Ink to Fin" is a Nomadic Grounds poetry insert. You may find it in a bag of coffee beans.

Thanks to all the editors, publishers, and readers who have supported this work.

ABOUT THE AUTHOR

LAUREN RUSSELL is the author of the chapbook *Dream-Clung, Gone* (Brooklyn Arts Press). Her poetry has appeared in *boundary 2, The Brooklyn Rail, jubilat,* and *Bettering American Poetry 2015,* among others. Russell is the recipient of fellowships from Cave Canem, VIDA/The Home School, the Wisconsin Institute for Creative Writing, and the National Endowment for the Arts. She is a research assistant professor and is assistant director of the Center for African American Poetry and Poetics at the University of Pittsburgh.

AHSAHTA PRESS

NEW SERIES

AHSAHTA PRESS

SAWTOOTH POETRY PRIZE SERIES

2002: Aaron McCollough, *Welkin* (Brenda Hillman, judge)

2003: Graham Foust, *Leave the Room to Itself* (Joe Wenderoth, judge)

2004: Noah Eli Gordon, *The Area of Sound Called the Subtone* (Claudia Rankine, judge)

2005: Karla Kelsey, *Knowledge, Forms, The Aviary* (Carolyn Forché, judge)

2006: Paige Ackerson-Kiely, *In No One's Land* (D. A. Powell, judge)

2007: Rusty Morrison, *the true keeps calm biding its story* (Peter Gizzi, judge)

2008: Barbara Maloutas, *the whole Marie* (C. D. Wright, judge)

2009: Julie Carr, *100 Notes on Violence* (Rae Armantrout, judge)

2010: James Meetze, *Dayglo* (Terrance Hayes, judge)

2011: Karen Rigby, *Chinoiserie* (Paul Hoover, judge)

2012: T. Zachary Cotler, *Sonnets to the Humans* (Heather McHugh, judge)

2013: David Bartone, *Practice on Mountains* (Dan Beachy-Quick, judge)

2014: Aaron Apps, *Dear Herculine* (Mei-mei Berssenbrugge, judge)

2015: Vincent Toro, *Stereo. Island. Mosaic.* (Ed Roberson, judge)

2016: Jennifer Nelson, *Civilization Makes Me Lonely* (Anne Boyer, judge)

This book is set in Apollo MT and DIN type
by Ahsahta Press at Boise State University.
Cover design by Quemadura. Cover artwork by Ashanti Africana.
Book design by Janet Holmes.

AHSAHTA PRESS

2017

JANET HOLMES, DIRECTOR

LINDSEY APPELL
PATRICIA BOWEN, *intern*
MICHAEL GREEN
KATHRYN JENSEN
COLIN JOHNSON
MATT NAPLES